HORST
Sixty Years of Photography

'In the Paris of the '30s, Horst set the style in fashion photography for decades' – *The Observer*

Horst P. Horst, born in Germany in 1906, became one of the world's most influential fashion photographers. Putting his unforgettable stamp on the international *Vogue* magazine of the 1930s and '40s, he soon became known not only for his extravagant fashion plates, but also for his exquisite still lifes and nudes, and his renowned portraits of such luminaries as Gertrude Stein, Katharine Hepburn, Jean Cocteau and Coco Chanel.

Horst: Sixty Years of Photography is a classic tribute to Horst's brilliant sixty-year career, bringing together 200 of his most outstanding photographs in a single, superbly produced volume.

Martin Kazmaier, who contributes the text, was born in Stuttgart in 1941. He is a television editor and a regular contributor to German periodicals on such subjects as art, opera and ballet. He has written several books on early French photography and the photography of the 1920s.

With 200 illustrations, 39 in colour and 161 in duotone

Horst, self-portrait, pencil and ink, 1942

HORST

Sixty Years of Photography

With a text by Martin Kazmaier
Edited by Richard J. Tardiff and Lothar Schirmer

*With 39 colour and 161 duotone plates,
29 black and white illustrations*

SCHIRMER ART BOOKS

The conceptual and practical difficulties encountered in the course of such an extensive project could not have been overcome without the help of many people. First of all, of course, the publishers would like to thank Horst for his active and enthusiastic encouragement throughout. We would like to thank Valentine Lawford for his constructive criticism; his great biography, *Horst. His Work and his World* (New York, 1984), remains an indispensable aid to any study of Horst's life and work, and each section of the present book is largely indebted to it. Richard J. Tardiff deserves special thanks for his untiring help in tracing and assembling the pictures.
Diana Edkins, Martin Kazmaier, Mikael Väisänen, Lisa Fonssagrives, Tina Summerlin, Rainer Wick, Ute Mundt and Anne de Margerie have all in their different ways contributed to the making of this book – they too receive our thanks.

Schirmer Art Books is an imprint of Schirmer/Mosel Verlag GmbH, Munich.
For trade information please contact: Schirmer Art Books, 112 Sydney Road,
Muswell Hill, London N10 2RN, England, or Schirmer/Mosel Verlag,
P. O. Box 401723, 80717 München, Germany, Fax 089/338695

A CIP catalogue record for this book is available from the British Library.

Translated from the German by Karen Williams
Text copyright © 1991 by Schirmer/Mosel Munich
This edition © 1991/1995 by Schirmer/Mosel Munich

Printed and bound in Germany
ISBN 3-88814-812-X
A Schirmer/Mosel Production

CONTENTS

Marina, Princess of Greece and Denmark, the
future Duchess of Kent, Paris, 1934

Horst P. Horst, Photographer

A woman in a flowing, light-coloured dress. Her right hand resting on a balustrade, her left casually at her waist. The classic pose. The dress is so long that it spills over the tapestry-laid marble steps. She stands in front of dark hangings, near a pillar. On the pillar a sparkle of light, gratuitous, but nevertheless powerful in its effect. Behind, a view into the drawing room.

Her eyes gaze wistfully into the distance. Madame is somewhat aloof; without being cold, she shows no interest in the world around her. Even the gentlemen in the drawing room draw no response. She is beautiful and knows it. She is Marina, Princess of Greece and Denmark, and the future Duchess of Kent. Horst P. Horst photographed her for *Vogue*. Fashion-conscious women in both the Old and New Worlds are captivated by such icons of elegance. The fair sex – for a man would never read *Vogue* – dreams of moving in highest society; highest society enjoys admiring its reflection, imagining the longing gazes of the fashionable women on whose coffee tables *Vogue* lies. Whilst concealing itself behind sheltering walls, society nevertheless wants to be seen.

Horst photographs his women as goddesses – almost unattainable, somewhat statuary and with Olympian composure. But his poses are not frozen. There were, in the thirties and forties, others who shared his approach. But his hand remains instantly recognizable: formal portraits replete with calm, distanced elegance.

'You see what you have done. You are a genius', said Diana Vreeland, who was to become, in the sixties, editor-in-chief of *Vogue*. She knew what she wanted. Once again he

Horst posing for George Hoyningen-Huene, Paris, 1930

Horst, photographed by Hoyningen-Huene, Paris, 1931

had created a photograph which bore his stamp, even without his striking signature. Horst means fashion and elegance in black-and-white, means studio atmosphere, means silhouette, means shadow. It means a pose so very much a pose that the result is unconscious ease – whether Horst has read Kleist's essay on the marionette or not.

He is not simply a fashion photographer. He is also a master of interiors, still lifes, plant photography, advertising and the early lifestyle photograph. But it is fashion, black and white, that people want from him.

How did you do that, Mr Horst? He is no naive artist. He is a craftsman, like Georges Braque, for example. He dislikes discussing the technical side of photography. He goes to the studio, where everything has already been prepared. By him, even, the night before. The lights are in place, the props selected. There is no dithering. Brief instructions to the model. No encouraging 'Baby, do it'. No music. Just concentration.

Be it the thirties, when models had to hold their poses, or the nineties, when photography is a matter of one thousandth of a second, the goal remains the same: 'To make people look good.' There was no mention of the word elegance during our conversations in Long Island and Manhattan.

8

Germany is far away, and with it the little town of Weissenfels-an-der-Saale, where 'Ironmongery, Stoves and Ovens' stood over his parents' shop. Solid middle class, neither particularly narrow-minded nor particularly cosmopolitan. A Biedermeier suite, five Meissen plates, a wealthy aunt in Weimar. The city of Schiller and Goethe lay nearby, but the Bauhaus remained remote, even though he wanted to be an architect. He was entranced by a young dancer living with his aunt in Weimar, not so much in love with her as with the *Zeitgeist* which manifested itself in her studies: modern German dance, an artistic way of life.

In Hamburg he was supposed to learn something useful. But his goal was Paris. He wrote to Le Corbusier and received a vague reply. He was far from enraptured by the architect's atelier. The master worked silently at his desk. Horst shuddered to discover that he was working on a project to demolish the elegant old Marais quarter in order to put up workers' apartment blocks.

Somewhere in Paris he met Baron George von Hoyningen-Huene, a Baltic aristocrat and well-known photographer working for *Vogue*. A difficult character. Irascible, good-natured, vegetarian, whimsical, a loner. He also went early to bed, quite something in Paris. Horst moved into his studio, assisted, posed.

There was ridicule from Cecil Beaton, the English dandy and society and fashion photographer with whom Horst remained in friendly competition throughout his life. He had been an art student until he started modelling hellenistic poses for the Baron. The blond German's repertoire included skiers and athletes, too! He was not particularly tall, but not short either; not the build of a bodyguard, perhaps, but extremely handsome and in superb condition. In Huene's studio he grew into his profession. Horst, who had never held a camera in his hands before (indeed, no one held cameras in those days; they stood on tripods), disappeared underneath the black cloth. He photographed, and sold his pictures to *Vogue*. The fact that he was young and beautiful played its part here, too. Photographers and chief editors were 'artists' and 'aesthetes', after all. He found his own style immediately. A sorcerer's apprentice. Even if Cecil Beaton maintained the opposite. And thus Horst Paul A.

Bohrmann from Saxony became a French photographer. French not just for the sake of fashion. French, too, in the tradition of studio photography as cultivated by Nadar and his atelier. French, too, in his choice of subjects. He learned the language easily. Actress, singer and society lady Yvonne Printemps, wife of successful popular author Sacha Guitry, taught him a Parisian accent.

The young publisher Condé Nast had bought *Vogue*, an American society magazine hailing from the previous century, in 1909. His aim was clear right from the start: *Vogue* was to be the fashionable journal for the international female world. Much more than just a fashion magazine. *House and Garden, Vanity Fair*, similarly published under the Condé Nast roof, addressed the same public. After the publication of American and British *Vogue*, *Vogue Française* finally appeared in 1921, fashion oracle and self-portrait of a society at which rich America stared.

Vogue illustrated women in fullest regalia; a portrait of society was thus painted which simultaneously showed fashions on sale to all. It was a time-honoured means of display. In the ancestral portrait galleries of the aristocracy, noble ladies and gentlemen flaunt their splendour as if having lived their entire lives simply for this one moment of sitting or standing as models. But what had once been signified by richness and rank of dress, family jewels and other signs of social position, was now expressed by fashionableness, by the feeling for style, as stated via a big name in Parisian *haute couture*. The popular society painters who – like Winterhalter – portrayed courtly ladies and gentlemen with photographic accuracy were now replaced by famous photographers. Such as Edward Steichen, whose artistic compositions could never quite conceal their descent from the easel, and Baron de Meyer, who flattered an international society with his soft lens. They remained examples to be emulated, but to *Vogue* their style was soon to appear too 'Edwardian'.

Aristocracy, art and fashion were in those days closely related. But Horst was interested in fashion only to the point of photographing it in his studio or, occasionally, in the salon of some society lady. Nor did he have much to do with the group of Surrealists proper. He was friends only with Dali and his muse, Gala. He met them at Coco Chanel's.

Horst and Natasha Paley in an underground film.
Photo: Hoyningen-Huene, Paris, 1932

Horst (left), and Hoyningen-Huene in Cecil Beaton's
country house. Photo: Cecil Beaton, Ashcombe, 1930

Mademoiselle was very much in love with the blond Horst. For her he felt only admiration, great admiration. Coco Chanel sought to shield him from her rivals, from her 'best friend' Misia Sert and from Schiaparelli, the Italian, as Chanel scornfully called her. Coco Chanel launched Cocteau, financially supported him, created outfits. Cocteau supplied fashion designs for *Harper's Bazaar*. Legendary all-round genius Christian Bérard also numbered amongst this circle of close friends. His drawings in *Vogue* were unmistakable, as too were his stage sets, and the décors for films such as *La Belle et la Bête* which transformed Cocteau's ideas into a magical work of art, an apotheosis of the black-and-white film. The Surrealists maintained their distance from the clique surrounding Cocteau. His affected manner and the company he kept – loutish genius Raymond Radiguet; Jean Marais, a shop boy, as Misia Sert put it – were too offensive for the serious artists. And if Horst, naturally rather reserved, failed to be at home in every sphere of art and society at once, could anyone else have succeeded? He therefore elected for only the most elevated of social circles.

Horst's Paris was neither the first arrondissement, nor the Quartier Latin, nor Montparnasse, nor even Montmartre, but a distinguished residential area, the seventh, not far from the Eiffel Tower and its extensive gardens. Not far, either, from the Place du Palais-Bourbon, where *Vogue* resided. Horst's Paris: the *Vogue* studio on the Champs Elysées,

11

charming acquaintances whose wealth did not intimidate him. Invitations to châteaux. Café terraces. Proust's world was making its adieus, but not without having itself photographed one last time in *Vogue*'s studio. Horst moved in circles to which even dollar millionaires had no access. Headed by Elsa Maxwell and Hemingway, they were too loud. He had friends who looked down haughtily on international café society. He was a frequent visitor at the home of the Vicomtesse de Noailles, whose family had produced many a general and cardinal. The Vicomte and his wife took almost no part in society life but, as lovers of art and music, held salons for a small circle. Sometimes in the beige drawing room with its futuristic furnishings by Horst's friend Jean-Michel Frank. They gave intimate private concerts and financed Buñuel's Surrealist masterpiece, *Un Chien Andalou.*

Horst was friends with writer Louise de Vilmorin, with Julien Green and his sister and, through his artist friend Bérard, with Gertrude Stein, collector and patroness of the arts. One day, at the Noailles' house, he met Count Visconti: *coup de foudre* and the start of a turbulent and subsequently lifelong friendship. Janet Flanner, Paris correspondent until the war for the influential *New Yorker*, became an important friend; she reviewed a tiny Horst exhibition in a sophisticated suburban gallery, which ended long before her article appeared, lauding the mastery of his pictorial composition and daringly tracing it back to his earlier work with wood and steel. At all events, and whether she was right or wrong, New York began talking about the talented young man from Germany for the first time.

Fashion and Surrealism: that meant Dali, Man Ray, Schiaparelli and many others besides. Although Horst does not rate as considerable his contribution to Surrealism, he shared the movement's aesthetic. He produced no Surrealist photos *per se*. He acknowledges an advertisement for Cartier jewelry as one of his few consciously Surrealist compositions. But the *trompe l'oeil* which he employed to sell the age-old theme of the hat, his compositions of hands, gloves and roses, the alchemistic glass balls he used to advertise cosmetics – these are all Surrealist works of art. Two shapely legs, their skin left even softer by a cream, are joined by a third, of wax.

A shimmering wax bath which leaves the lady even lovelier, even slimmer, evokes the slightly macabre memory of the anatomical waxworks which toured the fairgrounds of earlier days. Schiaparelli, who together with Dali created Surrealist fashions, he photographed inside a frame, as if in a mirror. He photographed a woman in an elegant evening dress by Madeleine Vionnet. Corals and shells create an underwater atmosphere to which the woman in the aquarium seems utterly indifferent. Above her, in a sublime cascade of folds, classical drapery defies its watery environment. Such compositions anticipated the surreal window displays of Hermès and Tiffany. Horst is no mannerist. Seldom does he select daring perspectives, seldom extreme, alienated details. He is sparing even with mirror effects. And the famous picture of the clown on tall stilts, with the long shadow? 'That was Diana Vreeland's idea. She wanted it like that.' He is not conceited.

Horst is not a magician but an illusionist. His studio substitutes for the world. With the right props, the right light, he creates an atmosphere, a personal ambience, before a few square metres of white screen in some New York or Paris studio. He was also one of the first to photograph against a light background. Usually, though, he chooses a chair, a console, a screen, or a Gobelin, a Fragonard, a Goya – as photographic enlargement. He works with plaster casts of antique statues, with consoles which in truth are merely boards, transformed through lighting into fashion accessories. He needs no rococo props for his kind of elegance. The modern, functional furniture of his friend Jean-Michel Frank looks thoroughly fashionable in his studio. Horst traces his ability to work so well with such makeshift scenery to his knowledge of carpentry and architecture.

Edward Steichen's famous photograph showed the barefooted dancer Isadora Duncan before the columns of the Parthenon. Horst photographed a model in the sculptural pleats of an evening gown by Alix. Two rolls of paper, to the left and right, and he had created the same impression of antiquity. Despite his ciphers, despite his props, Horst is no symbolist, no secretmonger. In Huene's studio home in Paris, in which Horst himself was later to live, stood the cast of a horse's head from the Acropolis, that definitive expression of the Ancient Greece which both men loved. Huene photographed Horst as the blond young god on his spirited steed. An almost identical horse's head appears in later pictures by

Horst in the pose of an ancient Greek horseman.
Photo: Hoyningen-Huene, Paris, 1932

Horst. Did he inherit Huene's horse? No, and nor had the parallel even struck him. He seldom leafs through his book of memories. He is a photographer, not a biographer. Rick Tardiff, his friend, manager, assistant and the critical eye supervising even the first prints, is the person to ask about such things.

Horst's studio sets began with an old, moth-eaten, velvet armchair in *Vogue*'s Paris studio. Coco Chanel brought her own chair with her, and later even a carved Pompadour screen. She hadn't been photographed for years. Indeed, she really only wanted to model her favourite dress, having seen it worn properly by none of her own mannequins. In the curve of the armchair the master of shadow modelled her face as flat and white, inimitable.

All is illusion. Beneath an ornamental lamp-post, Ginger Rogers floats in evening dress across a simple parquet floor. Her pose and the studio ventilator ensure her weightless grace. 'Shall we dance?' The Karajans pose, as if about to dash off. In a cabriolet or some madcap motor. It is impossible to tell that the photo was actually taken in Kitzbühel, for Horst worked here as in the studio. A later photo of the maestro, taken at his request in New York, shows Herbert von Karajan in tails, without orchestra, without audience, yet in an inimitable pose of sensitivity, as if standing before a world-class orchestra. Andy Warhol wanted to sit for the star photographer several times. He dragged statues and his favourite

14

Coco Chanel, Paris, 1937

Jacqueline, Vicomtesse de Ribes,
New York, 1953

dog along to the studio with him. Madame Jacqueline de Ribes, when still the society lady and not yet the fashion designer, came to Manhattan only briefly, for love. She found time enough to seek out Horst's studio, nevertheless. An elegant armchair on which she barely rests, on the mantelpiece a pair of classical torsos from an interiors shop: the fashionable lady in her home. A picture puzzle. For when Horst had to photograph within an elegant domestic ambience, he would banish everything intimate through his lighting. The home became the studio.

He is no more interested in alienation effects than bold perspectives. He is a classicist.

His props are brilliant ciphers, and nevertheless only stage sets. He can photograph plaster to look like marble, and marble to look like plaster. He buys his casts somewhere in the Quartier Latin. A papier-mâché lily, a cast after Houdon. His lighting elevates banality to a refined range of grey shades. He has a subtle feel for materials. He loves linen, wood, taffeta, less so velvet, which is too pompous for him. He can even photograph fur, the most difficult of all. Feathers he only really used in the case of Mistinguett, whom he captured in the classic pose of the revue star. All in white, with a bouquet of lilies, caressed by ostrich feathers. The big jewellers love the way he sets off their precious creations so effectively. Who could photograph pearls as Horst does – a silvery shimmer on black-and-white? He is

15

a pupil of Vermeer and Chardin. He is a magician of colour. He is a master of the still life. A flea-market in Paris. Single blooms. Even a traditional still life of game, with dead partridge and trophies of the hunt. Later, in the age of colour, he photographed porcelain for advertisements, as well as roses and parrot tulips, as brilliant as in the paintings of the great Flemish masters. The epoch-making *Vogue Book of Houses, Gardens, People*, which passed through many editions, he photographed entirely using natural light. He subtly exploited the given lighting effects. The morning sun can also be a powerful spotlight. The globe became a studio. One small detail posed a particular problem to stylization – the fact that even fashionable women have hands. He studied the position of the hands of antique statues in the Louvre, he consulted plaster casts, and Italian prints, with successful results. For awkwardness and mannerism are rarely found in his work. He has been spared the archness, the unnatural movement, the affectation of top models. He is a master of sheer elegance.

Horst's trademark is dramatic lighting. His colleagues used entire batteries of spotlights in trying to imitate him. Dramatic lighting? But that's nothing new, insists the master. All the great painters understood the principle – Caravaggio, Rembrandt, Vermeer.

First the set has to be right. Next comes the lighting. Then the model gets dressed and moves around the set, allowing Horst to familiarize himself with her walk. It is the lighting which creates the atmosphere. He uses a ceiling spotlight. That lends the photo something constructivist, a touch of Art Deco. The *Vogue* people were constantly demanding more drama. He gets dramatic effects with spotlights, as on a stage. He usually uses four, but naturally there are no fixed rules. He employs shutters in front of the spotlights to either reduce or open up the light, to bring out the detail of a dress. He has little interest in flat light. He wants to use light to change things, to shape them, by highlighting a profile, a structure, a detail of a silhouette.

When, in 1978, French *Vogue* invited Horst to photograph the collections, he used his old magic tools, the old wizardry. He succeeded in obtaining the same effects with a Rolleiflex. No one had worked with spotlights for years. He used the old equipment in the

 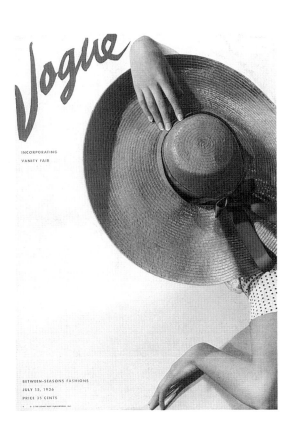

Vogue covers, photographed by Horst, 1936-41

Vogue studio, and the results were a huge success. Horst photographed exactly as before, but with a little more freedom. 'Fantastic', congratulated Yves Saint Laurent. Immediately everyone was copying Horst; soon no advertisement could do without spotlights. In Paris they were sold out.

Horst nevertheless avoids the play on shadow exploited by many of his colleagues and emulators. A shadow occasionally falls on a bright background. Among his imitators, however, the mannerism of the long shadow became routine. On the studio screen appeared silhouettes of scissor-sharp menace, supposed to be artistic.

Horst uses no filters. He is no camera fetishist. At the beginning he worked with the studio camera. Later with the more versatile Rolleiflex. Often he would only supply contact sheets, unable to decide which was the best shot. Usually he wouldn't even indicate cropping. Specks of dust and other details unwittingly captured on film he left to experienced retouchers. The darkroom was not his domain. He can be pleased that his collectors are more appreciative of such technical details than he is himself. There is a flourishing trade in first prints. Two years ago, in a New York gallery, they were fighting over the platinotypes.

What distinguishes a photo by Horst P. Horst from that of a colleague? Cecil Beaton usually moves in closer to his model; his photos appear fuller, some as if framed. Many of his portraits are taken against neutral backgrounds. He developed his own visual language for the pictures of the British royal family: luxury furnishings, hangings and the lush vegetation of paintings by Fragonard. Clarence Sinclair Bull produced portraits of the stars for MGM which were both magical and, at the same time, simple. His light is sweeter. He is pleasantly different from other studio photographers. In Horst P. Horst's era, *Vogue* alone employed more than a dozen well-known photographers and every stylistic extreme.

Such as Blumenfeld, who loved breathtaking action: Lisa Fonssagrives, Horst's favourite model, dances above the rooftops of Paris amongst the dizzying steel struts of the Eiffel Tower. And the other *Vogue* photographers who, like Horst, copied or were supposed to copy Edward Steichen's style. Nevertheless, Horst is quite different, at least in his portraits and fashion photography. It is not simply his famous light. He also maintains a certain distance from the camera, a distance which, together with his lighting, flatters even without filters. The differences between Horst and his colleagues are minimal. And yet Horst P. Horst is recognizable at a glance. Of course, the lens of a camera is impartial, objective, whether the eye behind it is cynical, bitter-sweet or ice-cold. But lighting, angle, distance and proximity express the photographer's attitude nevertheless. Photography is surface, wrote American essayist Susan Sontag. The viewer studies it and intuitively recognizes what lies beneath, the reality which it represents. Horst's photography is pure surface. The viewer attempts to fathom the relation between artist and model. Why is the Mona Lisa smiling? In many portrait photos it can be sensed which of the model's traits the photographer wished to capture. But Horst gives little away. He permits his models no excessive coquetry. He photographs unmoved; he makes no comment. Neither photographic nor autobiographic. Explanations are hard to extract from him. How did Gertrude Stein end up in the Balmain showroom? She is disguised, as always, as an ordinary woman; but beneath her small gilt chair may lie the shopping bag in which she will pick up a small Picasso on the way home. In the background a mannequin, artist friends. No indication of what had brought them all together. It was 1946, and Balmain had 'invited' Gertrude Stein to his country house. She called in on him now and again out of gratitude.

He photographed the ageing Louise Brooks, once Hollywood's Lulu, the vamp with the bob. She had been reduced to utter poverty, had only two cups left. But Horst formulates no charges. He leaves the verdict to the viewer. He photographed Misia Sert, the Parisian society lioness, once queen of international Venetian society, now sad and emaciated in front of a magnificent Veronese. The picture speaks for itself. No funerary gondola, no symbol. Grief on the surface, all the deeper. A rose is a rose is a rose, said Gertrude Stein. A photograph is surface.

Horst photographs the pose. 'Sit down'. He issues instructions, leaves nothing to chance. For the person in front of his camera, it is clear: this is the moment of truth. Only with Toscanini was the atmosphere so turbulent, so *allegro con spirito*, that he was able to pho-

Misia Sert in the Galleria dell'Accademia, Venice, 1947

Arturo Toscanini, New York, 1941

Tamara Toumanova, at the age of 15, Monte Carlo, 1931

tograph the maestro twelve times without him noticing. Quite the opposite with Maria Callas. In the New York apartment you could cut the air with a knife. For one instant Horst played animal trainer. He was delighted to get out in one piece. The photograph was not published.

His first snapshot: Monte Carlo, 1931. The Casino also housed the rooms in which Diaghilev's ballet company was training. Tamara Toumanova, the beautiful baby ballerina, was sitting on the steps. He clicked. Such spontaneity was rare. He preferred to have everything under control. The shadow of the ridge of a nose, the sparkle of an eye, the hand on the back of the chair. Even his snapshots are controlled, far from the style of modern fashion photographers, who shoot metres of film in order to select the best shots later. Horst never took photographs during a fashion show – only ever before or after. His pictures of the huge gala balls were no snapshots, either. The Dominos and Dubarrys had to come to his studio.

There is, however, one very distinctive type of Horst snapshot. The props and the lighting are ready. The model poses. Several well-planned photographs are taken. But then, right at the end, something unpredictable happens. In the case of Martha Graham, whom he photographed in 1990, it was when the dancers waiting for their class stormed into the ballet room. The sudden creation of a photo full of life. Or he clicks out of impatience, as with Dick Cavett, who kept him waiting too long after a show. The result could not have been bettered.

Groups he photographs almost solely for advertisements. They have no place in his fashion photography. His women are solitary and proud. In 1971, for the catalogue of a well-known New York model agency, he assembled the actress Silvana Mangano, the French writer François-Marie Banier and the black pop singer Sterling St. Jacques in front of the studio camera. 'Mangano looks out of the corner of her eye, her face partially shaded, her mouth sensuous. Young Banier, thin-lipped and narrow-eyed, looks at her, in profile. And then the handsome singer with full lips. That's how the tension is developed.'

As in Paris, so later in New York: Horst knew everyone. But he did not photograph everyone. Aristocrats, artists, beauties, the Vanderbilts – all crowded in front of his camera. Not to mention the actors, singers and other celebrities who, following their triumphs in New York, had to be photographed for *Vogue*. Such as Lotte Lehmann as the Marschallin at the Met.

Horst was not someone who just took people's pictures. His studio had to be sought out. Horst is not the man with the camera recording social events. Photography is not even his hobby, and he is certainly not a photographic reporter like Weegee, the Austrian in New York. In his home in Long Island there may not even be a camera to be found.

For a long time Horst had a beautiful studio, taken over from a painter friend, in a 'tower block'. Here, too, he was at the very top. But then, after several years, he had to leave the apartment because he was using it for commercial purposes. He now rents a studio. Unusually, he photographed his friend Truman Capote in the latter's own home. There, in his city apartment on the East River, near the United Nations, the famous picture with the snake was taken. Capote was the most photographed author of his generation. At another sitting, in typically American style, he wanted to be photographed with the presents of rich friends and other trophies. He had arranged his favourite photos, in silver frames, on a table. They were all by Richard Avedon. Capote was never lost for a mean trick.

Horst was discreet. He even let a Garbo portrait go by. Garbo, as was well known, did not wish to be photographed in private. On this particular day he was photographing his guests, including Edith Sitwell, the eccentric with the face like thunder. But he photographed around Greta Garbo; a large hat, a vague profile and a somewhat pointed nose are only seen from a distance, under the pergola. In 1950, the future Jackie Kennedy was *Vogue* débutante of the year. Being not only beautiful but also very ambitious, she took part in *Vogue*'s 'Prix de Paris', a writing competition for women college students. Naturally, she won – and that from well over a thousand entrants. The winner was invited to work for *Vogue* for a year in New York and Paris. It was an opportunity Jackie had to forgo, at her stepfather's wish; she knew and loved Paris, and he didn't want her becoming too much of a Parisienne. The first honour awarded the winner, however, was a flight to New York, to be photographed by Horst P. Horst for *Vogue.*

Horst was captivated by her girlish beauty, admired her and photographed her, together with her sister, for a sweater advert.

Horst photographed all the First Ladies of the post-war period. At the invitation of the White House. He was friends with President Truman. He knew him from his army days.

Mr Horst, who did you not enjoy photographing? Marlene Dietrich. She came to his studio – in a 'Look out, here I come' manner – and demanded the special lighting which Josef von Sternberg had discovered and which highlighted her cheek bones – her old trick. But Horst photographed the way he wanted. He is a hypnotist. Barely were the contacts ready than she ordered dozens of prints. For he had succeeded in rendering her face young and unwrinkled, with a flattering nose. The light came from below. For Horst the matter was thereby closed.

Duran Duran, the English pop group, wanted to sit for a record cover. And there they sat, with blow-dried haircuts. 'One of my most boring photographs'. They refused to be played with. Then Tom Wolfe, author of *Bonfire of the Vanities.* Vanity itself. He came to the studio dressed as a provincial playboy in a white suit and believed it elegant. He refused to be told anything different. Horst found his mannerisms irritating. But it had to be, for

Greta Garbo (right), Sir Osbert Sitwell and Mab Wilson on the
terrace of Horst's house, 1949

Vogue. He made an entire series of Warhol, who wanted to be ennobled by his acclaimed colleague. Warhol was too commercial for Horst. But Warhol would have brought even his bedroom into the studio in order to collect himself in photographs.

Mapplethorpe, who learned so much from Horst, was another story. He was the friend of wealthy photo collector Sam Wagstaff. He bought first prints. Horst photographed Mapplethorpe and Mapplethorpe photographed Horst. Out of politeness. Mapplethorpe was too much at home in the New York 'scene' for Horst's liking; Horst P. Horst's motto, delivered in German, with a wink, is 'Immer anständig bleiben' – 'Always remain respectable'. As they used to say in Weissenfels. He photographed Bette Davis several times, officially. The young Jane Fonda was not yet an actress when he photographed her in Long Island. A snapshot of the young Bergman, and an armchair pose for *Vogue* of the mature actress. He remains friends with Katharine Hepburn even today.

Film held no attraction for him. In Paris he found 'le cinéma' silly, and sillier still the audiences who trooped to the movies in their Sunday best. In the studio, every woman wanted to be photographed as a film star.

Quite different, then, his friend Hoyningen-Huene, who, after a Hollywood visit, posed for Horst's camera in the guise of a tycoon, wearing a monocle like MGM's Irving Thalberg. The Baron later went over entirely to film, as colour consultant to George Cukor.

Horst was unfamiliar with the early German film masterpieces such as *Die freudlose Gasse* and *Metropolis*, films from the days when the screen had elemental power, and thus he was unfamiliar with their dramatic lighting. They never came to Weissenfels. Even if they had, he wouldn't have gone. Nothing would divert him from his course.

One of his most famous photos: the Mainbocher corset. The nude seen from behind has always been a prominent theme of French art. With or without a corset. Ingres' *Bather* in the Louvre. Then Charles Nègre, the subtle artist-photographer: a nude from behind against a drapery screen, 1842. Degas, the Impressionists – whom did the subject escape? The 'queens of hearts' of the last century were happy to be photographed from behind, naked or with a corset. Man Ray took up the theme: woman as violin. Salvador Dali loved the motif. Fashion designer Moschino painted a large question mark on his model's back.

Paris was the city of lingerie, of the corset. For the *boulevardier* in tails and top hat, there was no eroticism without button-boots and bodices. Chanel condemned the corset, but it came back into fashion before the war. 'I had never photographed a corset before. It wasn't easy. The light in the photo is more complex than you think. It looks as though there is only one light source. But there were reflectors and extra spotlights as well. I don't know how I did it. I couldn't repeat it. It was created by emotion.'

It was to be the last photograph Horst took in Paris before the war. The intimacy with which the model leans forward, the elegant hairstyle, the light which highlights the dark side of her beautiful back – the Mainbocher corset is charged with sadness and restrained eroticism.

'I worked until four in the morning, packed my bags, took the seven o'clock train and boarded the *Normandie*. She sank two days after reaching New York.'

Adieu, la France. Unexpectedly, it was as if American *Vogue* had been waiting for him. He integrated himself quickly and soon had the best connections. For instead of being

Robert Mapplethorpe's portrait of Horst, New York, 1986

deported to Germany, he became an American soldier, rapidly gained the higher ranks and was allowed to do in the army what he did otherwise: take photographs. Admittedly no countesses, no *haute couture*. During this period he began photographing plant life. A maple leaf in a glass. Washington 1942.

He photographed other leaves, plants, barks, crystals: *Patterns from Nature*, 1944. At the end, kaleidoscopic reflections of ornamental leaves, photographs in simple repetition, giving a – very American – patchwork-quilt effect. 'They are intended to serve as inspiration for textiles, carpets, ceramics.' Modern design with modern means.

He knew Blossfeldt's early plant photography. At this time he 'belonged' to *Vogue*, but was nevertheless allowed, by way of exception, to publish his book. He was a poor soldier. He won the war as an artist.

Then Condé Nast again. *Vogue* wanted star photographers. But star behaviour was out of the question. Independent photographers? The editors felt they were the true artists of photography; the man who had to creep under the black cloth was, in their eyes, little more

25

than an assistant. You had to turn a fashion magazine inside out to find the name of the photographer. Which wasn't always printed anyway. Not so with Horst P. Horst. As with an outfit by his friend Chanel, you can tell instantly who it's by.

Following the Allied victory, Condé Nast believed his magazines could play an even greater role in propagating American fashion and the American way of life. Girls who were young, beautiful, happy, spontaneous. At the same time, however, a dreadful prudishness prevailed. The girl in the itsy-bitsy bikini knew why she hardly dared leave the locker room: photographs were to be attractive without being suggestive. A thousand compromises: bathing fashions, but mannequins with towels over their heads, like mummies.

Horst was now forced to photograph through keyholes, a voyeur. Pictures were to look friendly and direct, like snapshots. But such photographs required even greater preparation, even more concentration, from the model as well as the photographer. Colour, meanwhile, had also come into play. The covers of American *Vogue* show that even Horst P. Horst did not always succeed in squaring the circle. Models were now also to be photographed in the street, as by Richard Avedon for French *Vogue*. Avedon even had a bus at his disposal, with rooms for mannequins, make-up and clothes. Horst photographed in front of Philip Johnson's daring glass architecture on Broadway. His mannequin poses on a terrace, floats, absolved of all banality, purified. The skyscraper as gigantic studio prop.

Does Horst P. Horst value naturalness? His photos are mainly stills, but quite different from those of Hollywood. There they are loud, colourful, often featuring monstrous props. In Horst's work, the quiet elegance of the connoisseur prevails. The stars, as Louise Brooks once said, live as stills in the imagination of their public.

Garbo, gazing mysteriously into the camera. Captured poses, divine images of the cinema. Horst's photographs have an artificial naturalness. He has a certain nonchalance. The composition is more important than the smile on the lips. 'Say "cheese"' is not one of his commands. The silhouette smiles, the shadow smiles. 'How do you want my hair?' asks the star. 'I'm supposed to be photographing you, not your hair.' His *Vogue* photos had nothing in common with the grotesque, doll-like publicity shots which Hollywood required.

Horst P. Horst, you are one of the most famous fashion photographers. *'Um Himmelswillen!'* ('For heaven's sake!') he says, in a mixture of American and drawing-room Tyrolese accent. Fashion is not his world. He can often barely still recall who designed a particular evening gown or flimsy day dress. Here, in particular, the law of demand ruled the day. In the beginning, in Paris, he saw himself as a society portraitist. Then came the professional models. Here, too, he sought personalities. He is not cynical, and he remembers almost every mannequin.

Lisa Fonssagrives, 'Penn's wife'. She had married his respected colleague, Irving Penn. Her body was beautiful, her movements perfect, for she was a dancer. He took a number of nudes which were not published – and certainly not in *Vogue*. Horst is an extreme aesthete. In Paris he discovered Ludmilla, his Lud, who was living in a houseboat on the Seine at the time, and whose mouth *Vogue* initially found too Slavonic. After becoming an enormous success she ran off with a lion-tamer.

He worked with Suzy Parker, the vivacious model, in Kitzbéhel and elsewhere, including for advertising. Sweet Suzy was too unruly for him. She later became a film actress; the vivacity she showed in front of his camera would not, he feels, have harmed her on the screen. Then came Veruschka. Horst is not the sort who claims to have discovered everything. But he discovered her. He was looking for someone to model bathing fashions in *Vogue*. He wanted a new face. He met the young countess in society, spoke to her. She offered her services, on one condition: she had to be named. And thus a top model was born. Diana Vreeland, Veruschka, Horst: a winning trio. All of his girls are more to him than mere clothes hangers.

From his city office, high up in an elegant tower – the 'Royale', with three doormen – he looks out over the beautiful roofscape of the Upper East Side. Below, the view drops to a street of magnificent plane trees. Star florist Renny also has rooms here. Horst has only ever lived right at the top or right at the bottom, half in the garden, where the curtains give way to flower beds. Or with only the heavens above him. Never in the middle, among other people. He thereby lets slip an unintentional clue to his character.

27

Horst and Suzy Parker on the way to Badgastein.
Photo: Valentine Lawford, Salzburg, 1952

He earned well. Shortly after the war he was able to buy a huge plot of land in Long Island, part of the park accompanying the – by then run-down – residence of Tiffany, the jeweller. For this he had to part with dearly loved works of art from Paris – a Picasso, for example. Costly presents from Coco Chanel he kept. His eclectic taste lends much its distinctive character. The wooden bungalow, white and Mediterranean, based on his own designs, is small and not built for eternity. His model was the house in Tunisia whose construction he had supervised for Hoyningen-Huene. The house with the pergola is, more accurately, an accent in the park. Here Garbo once sat. Over there, Truman Capote used to walk his bulldog along the river. Christopher Isherwood and Erich Maria Remarque have both been here. Over here Christian Dior froze in his long cowled coat. There Edith and Osbert Sitwell sat and were even photographed. Salvador Dali suggested surrealist plantations in the two streams where classic green vegetation now floats. The newly planted park was not classical enough for Cecil Beaton. Even so, it has a main axis, not too geometric; further away, before the line of trees, stands a large marble urn full of geraniums.

Horst feels at home in Long Island's social sphere. Yet he takes little part in society life. His literary and personal association with English diplomat Valentine Lawford dates back over almost half a century. They have written books, conceived articles and undertaken

28

Horst's Picasso in his New York apartment; vase and lamp designed by Diego Giacometti, 1939

Horst's house at Oyster Bay, Long Island – view from the terrace into the park, 1990.

long trips. Andy Warhol had his factory, in which he spread holy terror. Horst has his own type of family. He is surrounded by friends. He may not act the brave hero, defiantly ignoring American puritanism. But in this society you need to be as noble-minded as he is if you are to move in the highest circles without a sham wife at your side.

He has always been well-liked in society. Once in Paris, now in New York. He is American through and through. A trace of American colours his English. He wears a corduroy shirt with mother-of-pearl buttons. His trademarks include a cowboy scarf, if necessary a bow-tie. He drinks whisky in moderate quantities. He is not really an intellectual. Or he is good at concealing it. Another sign of a true gentleman. He has a great deal of charm and the famous Saxon wit. Now and again a playful wink, something he never allows his camera.

Horst's photography has been tied to the studio. A naked girl on a beach would at least have made a change. A naked boy even more so. At one time, he wanted to give up and buy a farmhouse in Austria. Then, in 1962, Diana Vreeland appeared at *Vogue*. She freed him from the yoke of fashion. He was able to travel, photograph interiors and rich people. His point of pride. No artificial light. No assistant other than Valentine Lawford, who wrote the commentaries. Rooms were to be photographed from the intimate viewpoint of their inhabitants. He showed details, avoided symmetrical alignments, included favourite chairs. He had nothing against a little disorder at times: a bouquet of flowers no longer quite fresh, cushions plumped to less than regimental stiffness. Even back in his Paris years he had spoken of the acceptability of 'a little mess' – a dirty ashtray, for example. Although I've never yet found one. Or did *Vogue*'s retouchers magic it away?

He photographed the home of Emilio Pucci, his boldly coloured prints modelled by mannequins on the roof of his Florentine palazzo. He visited Baron Philippe de Rothschild, whose second wife, Pauline, was American. He couldn't admire her enough. She devised the theme of 'Wine in Art'. He photographed the American painter Cy Twombly in his old Roman palazzo – entirely spontaneous images of an unconventional lifestyle. There are relaxed scenes, too: a young lord rummaging through the bric-à-brac in one of the rooms of his newly inherited property.

These, then, were the best years at *Vogue*. After the departure of Diana Vreeland he worked almost exclusively for *House and Garden*. It would seem that, behind the scenes of a magazine like *Vogue*, not everything is as civilized as its glossy cover suggests.

Horst is one of the best-organized people I have ever met – a true Prussian on that score. In the tumult of New York he manages to be absolutely punctual. No one knows how he does it, but he gets from Long Island to his studio all the same. Suddenly he's there, out of the blue. He enjoys the scope of his professional activities more than ever. Advertising, with and without fashion. Flowers and still lifes, for private clients and porcelain manufacturers. He occasionally still works in Paris, too. In 1990 he flew Concorde to photograph Princess Stéphanie of Monaco; he works a lot with Paloma Picasso. Fashion photography is naturally subject to the ups and downs of fashion itself. But class and style are still instantly recognizable. And that's Horst P. Horst. He is a genius. '*Um Himmelswillen!*', he would say, with a playful wink.

Horst in his studio, New York, 1984/85
Photo: Johann D. Mayr

1 Still life, Paris, 1933

2 Coco Chanel, Paris, 1937

3 Mistinguett, Paris, 1934

4 Louise de Vilmorin, Paris, 1937

5 Mme Jean Larivière posing as a figure from a Goya painting, Paris, 1935

6 Baron Nicolas de Gunzburg, Paris, 1934

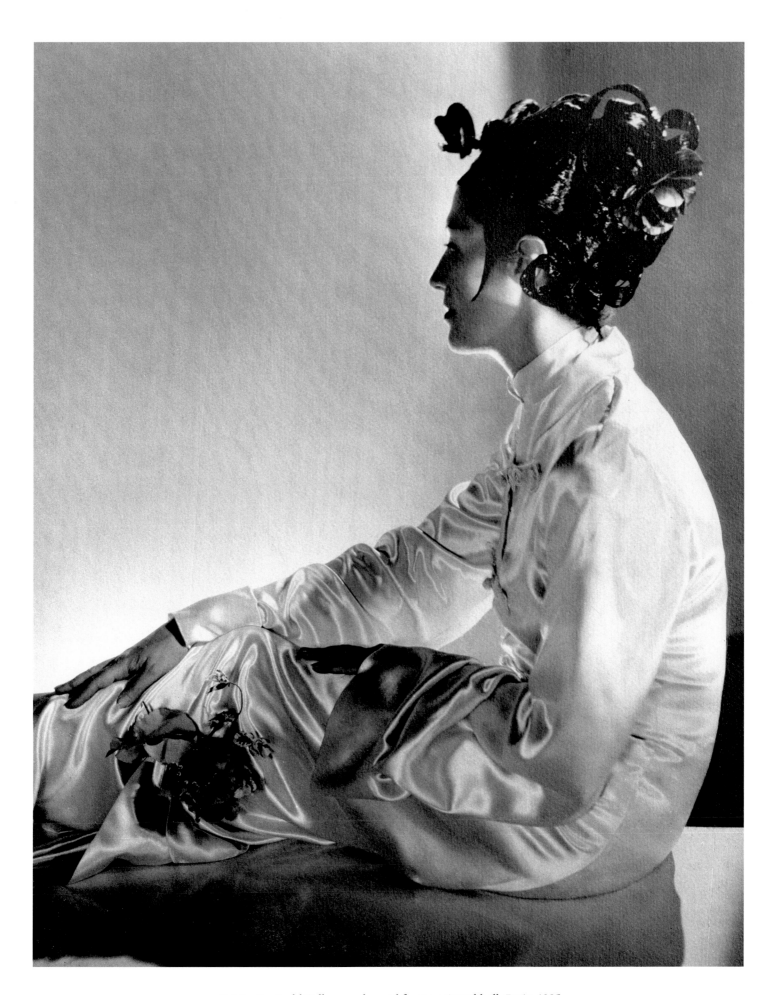

7 Mrs Reginald Fellowes, dressed for an oriental ball, Paris, 1935

8 The Mainbocher corset, Paris, 1939

9 Fashion shot, New York, 1937

10 Lisa Fonssagrives, New York, 1939

11 Marie-Laure, Vicomtesse de Noailles, Paris, 1935

12 Joan Crawford, New York, 1938

13 'I love you' – Lisa Fonssagrives with hat by Balenciaga and gloves by Boucheron, Paris, 1938

14 'White Sleeve', fashion shot with Doris Zelensky, Paris, 1936

15 Costume designs by Salvador Dali for his ballet *Bacchanale*, Paris, 1939

16 Helen Bennett, fashion shot, Paris, 1936

17 Helen Bennett, fashion shot, Paris, 1938

18 Elsa Schiaparelli, Paris, 1934

19 Advertisement for Bergdorf Goodman, New York, 1935

20 Marina, Princess of Greece and Denmark, the future Duchess of Kent, Paris, 1934

21 Evening gown by Alix, Paris, 1938

22 Bette Davis, New York, 1938/39

23 Ginger Rogers, New York, 1935

24 Luchino Visconti, Paris, 1936

25 Christian Bérard working on a screen for Edward Molyneux (left), Paris, 1933

26 George Hoyningen-Huene, Paris, 1934

27 Fashion shot, Paris, 1936

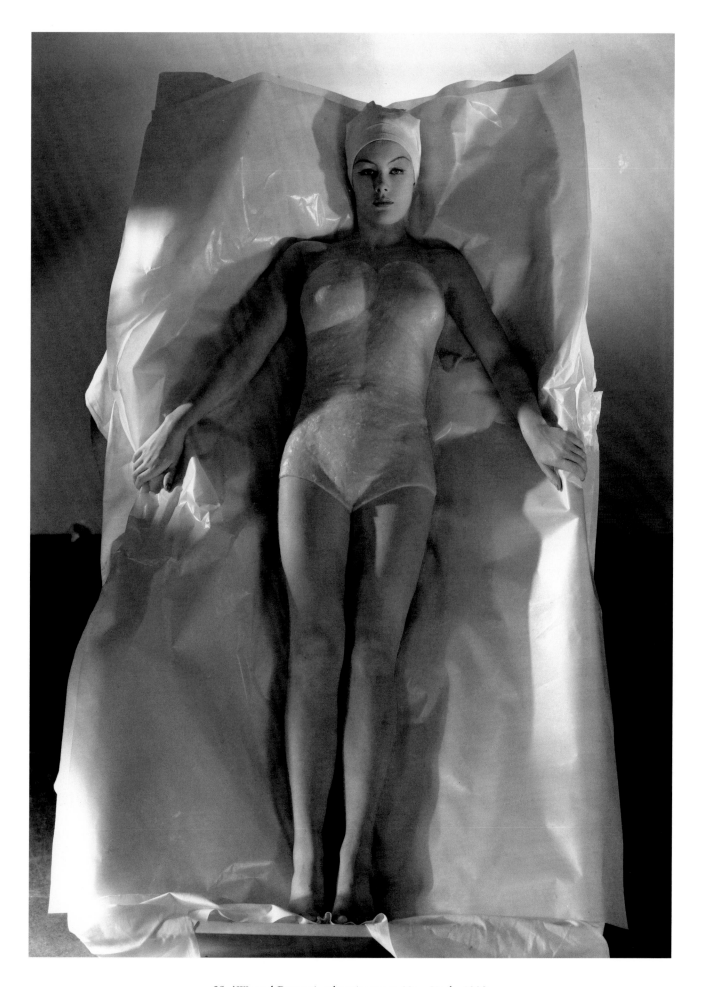

28 `Waxed Beauty', advertisement, New York, 1938

29 Barbara Hutton, New York, 1939

30 Nude, New York, 1939

31 Cover for *Vogue*, Paris, 1938/39

32 Nude, New York, 1940

33 *'Trompe l'oeil'*, still life with hat, Paris, 1938

34 Janet Flanner and Noel Murphy, Orgeval, France, 1933

35 Janet Flanner, Paris, 1931

36 Fashion shot, London, 1936

37 Noel Coward, Paris, 1934

38 Cole Porter, Paris, 1934

39 Katharine Hepburn, Hollywood, 1935

40 Henri Cartier-Bresson, Delphi, 1938/39

41 Christian Bérard (left) and George Hoyningen-Huene, Monte Carlo, 1932

42 Still life, New York, 1937

43 Estrella Boissevain, fashion shot, New York, 1938

44 'Electric Beauty', Paris, 1939

45 Clay sculpture, Acoma, New Mexico, 1947/48

46 Gala Dali, New York, 1943

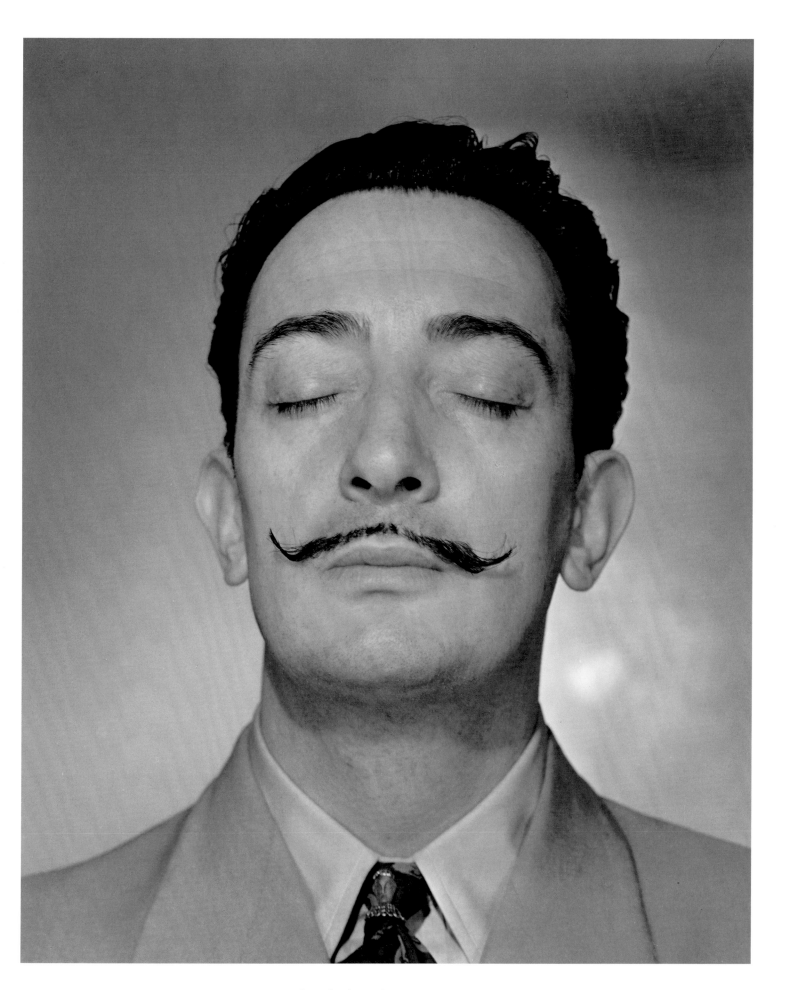

47 Salvador Dali, New York, 1943

48 Muriel Maxwell, New York, 1940

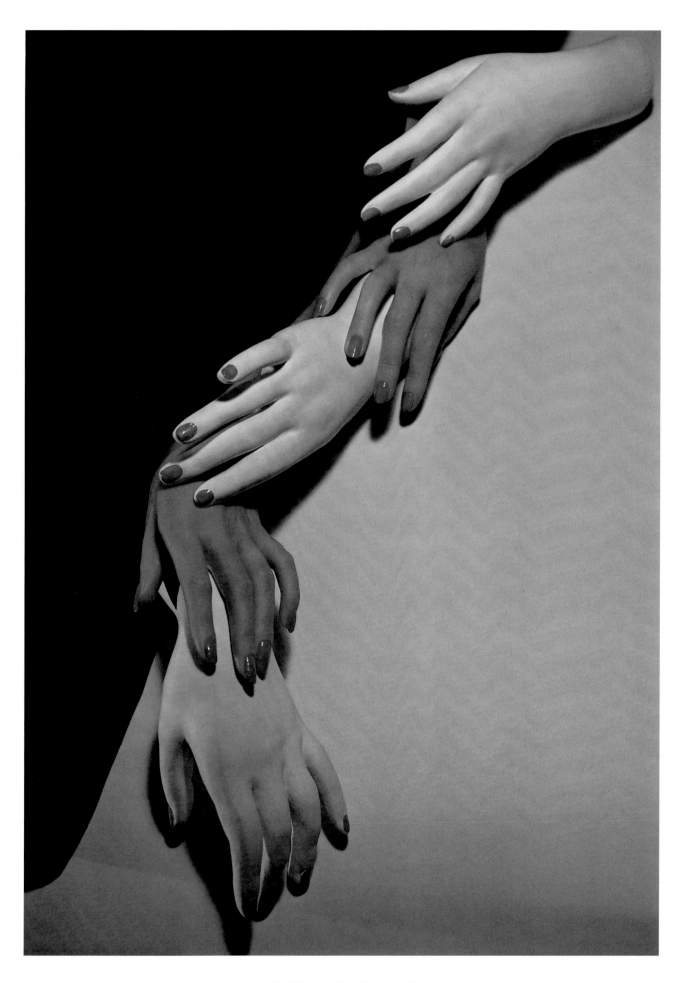

49 'Hands', New York, 1941

50 Surrealist still life, advertisement, New York, 1941

51 Lisa Fonssagrives with turban, New York, 1940

52 Lisa Fonssagrives' hands, New York, 1941

53 *'Odalisque'*, New York, 1943

54 Merle Oberon, New York, 1942

55 Myrna Loy, New York, 1942

56 Veronica Lake, New York, 1941

57 Gloves, New York, 1947

58 Lisa Fonssagrives, cover of *Vogue*, 1 September 1940

59 Loretta Young, New York, 1941

60 Marlene Dietrich, New York, 1942

61 Evening gown by Schiaparelli, New York, 1940

62 Still life, New York, 1944

63 Gene Tierney, New York, 1940

64 *Richardia Africana*, plant still life, New York, 1945

65 Torso by Mestrovic , Metropolitan Museum, New York, 1947

66 Paulette Goddard, New York, 1942

67 Fashion shot, New York, 1947

68 Fashion shot, New York, 1942

69 Lingerie by Dorian Leigh, New York, 1946

70 Alicia Markova, New York, 1941

71 Mme Maxime de la Falaise, fashion shot, Paris, 1949

72 Cecil Chapman and Adele Simpson, fashion shot, New York, 1948

73 Black bodice, fashion shot, New York, 1948

74 Maria Laudomia Hercolani-Del Drago, fashion shot, New York, 1948

75 The Duchess of Windsor, Waldorf Astoria Hotel, New York, 1943

76 Harry S. Truman, Washington, 1945

77 Edith Sitwell, New York, 1948

78 Fragment of a Persian sculpture, Persepolis, Iran, 1949

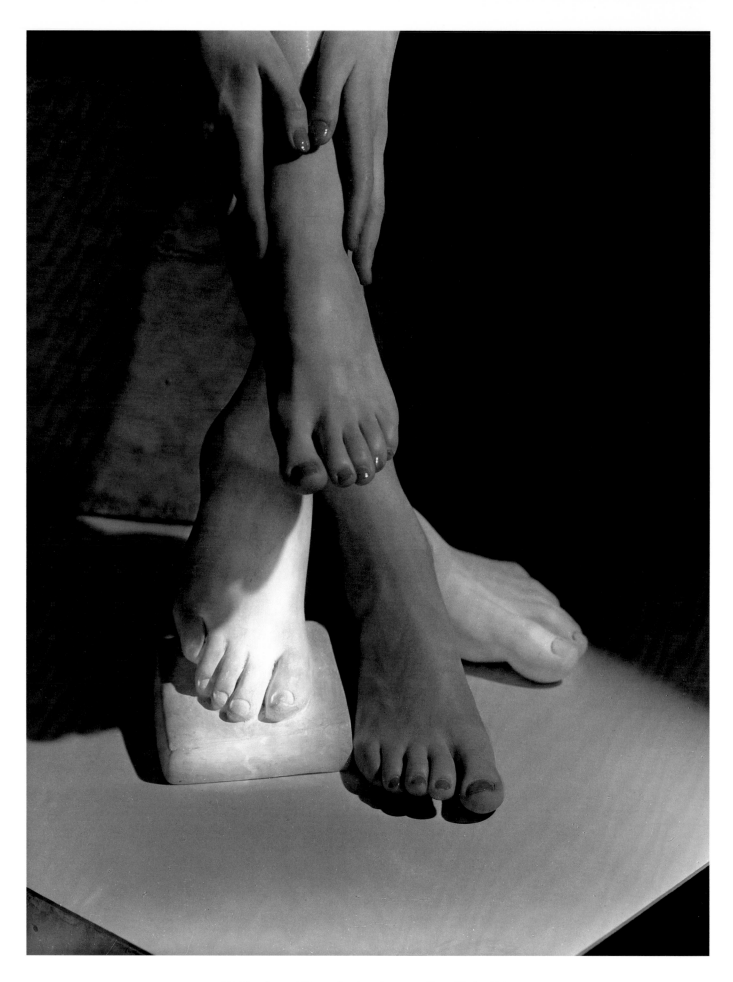

79 'Barefooted Beauty', advertisement, New York, 1941

80 Advertisement with Carmen, New York, 1946

81 Gertrude Stein, Paris, 1946

82 Carl Erickson drawing Gertrude Stein and Horst, Paris, 1946

83 Gertrude Stein at a Balmain fashion show; in the background, Rosamond Bernier and Carl Erickson, Paris, 1946

84 Valentine Lawford, England, 1948

85 Still life, New York, 1946

86 José Clemente Orozco, Mexico City, 1941

87 'Food to aid Europe', New York, 1947

88 Salvador Dali, New York, 1948/49

89 Richard Tyler, New York, 1946

90 Yul Brunner, New York, 1949

91 Burgess Meredith, New York, 1946

92 Jessica Tandy, New York, 1946

93 Diamante Boschetti, Villa Barbaro, Maser/Treviso, 1947

94 Marlene Dietrich and her daughter Maria Riva, New York, 1947

95 Jean Cocteau, Venice, 1947

96 Jean Marais, Venice, 1947

97 Bronze statue of Maria of Burgundy at the tomb of Maximilian, Imperial church, Innsbruck, 1951/2

98 Shepherd boy, Iran, 1949

99 Dome complex in the living quarters of the Ali Kapu Palace, Isfahan, Iran, 1949

100 Lisa Fonssagrives in a design by Pierre Balmain, New York, 1953

101 Nude, New York, 1953

102 Fashion shot, New York, 1943

103 Silver tea set, Oyster Bay, Long Island, 1952

104 'Triangle', study of a nude, New York, 1953

105 Lillian Marcuson, fashion shot, New York, 1950

106 Nina de Voe, fashion shot, New York, 1951

107 Cover for *House and Garden*, New York, 1951

108 Still life, Oyster Bay, Long Island, 1950

109 Fashion shot, Oyster Bay, Long Island, 1950

110 Still life with tulips, Oyster Bay, Long Island, *c.*1950

111 Evelyn Tripp in a design by Charles James, New York, 1951

112 Maria Stein, Tyrol, 1952

113 Alberto Moravia, Rome, 1958

114 Luchino Visconti, Rome, 1953

115 Maria Callas, New York, 1952

116 Eliette and Herbert von Karajan, Kitzbühel, 1954

117 Herbert von Karajan, New York, 1957/58

118 Lilli Palmer, New York, 1950

119 Ingrid Bergman, Paris, 1958

120 Gore Vidal, New York, 1953

121 Lisa Fonssagrives, fashion shot, New York, 1951

122 Irving Penn, New York, 1951

123 Yves Saint Laurent at Dior's, Paris, 1958

124 In the Forum Romanum, Rome, 1952

125 Giacomo Manzú, in his garden at Ardea, near Rome, 1958

126 Male nude, 1952

127 Tina Leser, fashion shot, New York, 1950

128 Jacqueline Bouvier, later Kennedy-Onassis, and her sister Lee, later Canfield-Radziwill, New York, 1958

129 Jane Fonda, Oyster Bay, Long Island, 1959

130 'After the party', Rome, 1951

131 In Cy Twombly's Roman palazzo, 1965

132 Cy Twombly and his wife Tatyana, Rome, 1965

133 Cy Twombly, Rome, 1965

134 View from the Hall of Mirrors in the Amalienburg, Nymphenburg Palace
gardens, Munich, 1965

135 Franco Zeffirelli, New York, 1961/62

136 Marisa Berenson, fashion shot, New York, 1965

137 Still life with flowers and Böcklin, Oyster Bay, Long Island, 1959

138 Fashion shot, Paris, 1960

139 Lingerie advertisement, New York, 1963

140 Veruschka von Lehndorf, New York, 1964

141 Marienburg Castle, Würzburg, 1965

142 Galanos fashions, New York, 1965

143 Tatiana, Princess Moritz of Hessen and her horse, Panker Palace, Lütjenburg, Holstein, 1967

144 Fashion shot, New York, 1962

145 Veruschka von Lehndorf, fashion shot, Hawaii, 1965

146 Papier-mâché iris, New York, 1968

147 Fashion shot, New York, 1961/62

148 Suzy Parker, fashion shot, Nassau, 1963

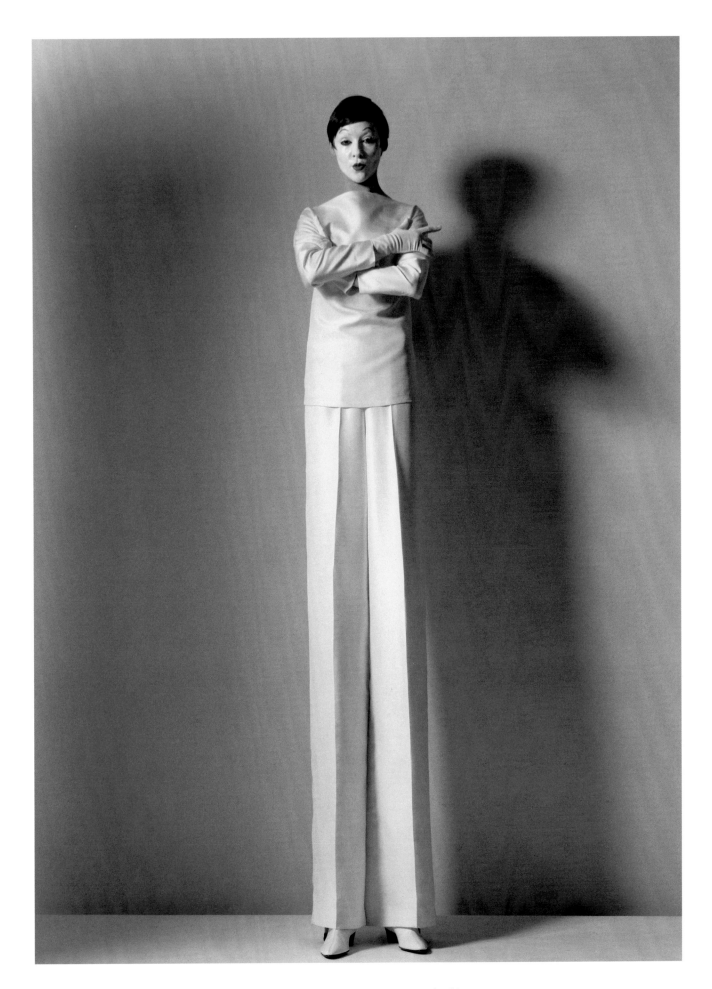

149 Fashion shot, New York, 1963/64

150 St Basil's Cathedral, Red Square, Moscow, 1975

151 Paloma Picasso in a design by Yves Saint Laurent, Paris, 1979

152 Silvano Mangano, François-Marie Banier and Sterling St. Jacques,
New York, 1971

153 W.H. Auden, New York, 1970

154 Louise Brooks, Rochester, New York, 1979

155 Robert Wilson, New York, 1977

156 Gilbert & George, Oyster Bay, Long Island, *c.*1976

157 Yves Saint Laurent fashions, Paris, 1979

158 Roy Lichtenstein in his studio, East Hampton, New York, 1978

159 Fashion shot, Paris, 1979

160 Daks fashions, New York, 1988

161 Shoulder bags, Paris, 1979

162 Truman Capote, New York, 1973

163 Yves Saint Laurent fashions, Paris, 1979

164 Patrick Kelly, New York, 28 April 1989

165 Daniel Duell of the New York City Ballet, in a costume by Ben Benson for Peter Martins' *Calcium Light Night*, New York, 1979

166 Claude Montana fashions, Paris, 1979

167 Nude, New York, 1982

168 Brooke Shields, Westbury Gardens, New York, 1984

169 Tulips, Oyster Bay, Long Island, 1989

170 Tom Wolfe, New York, 1983

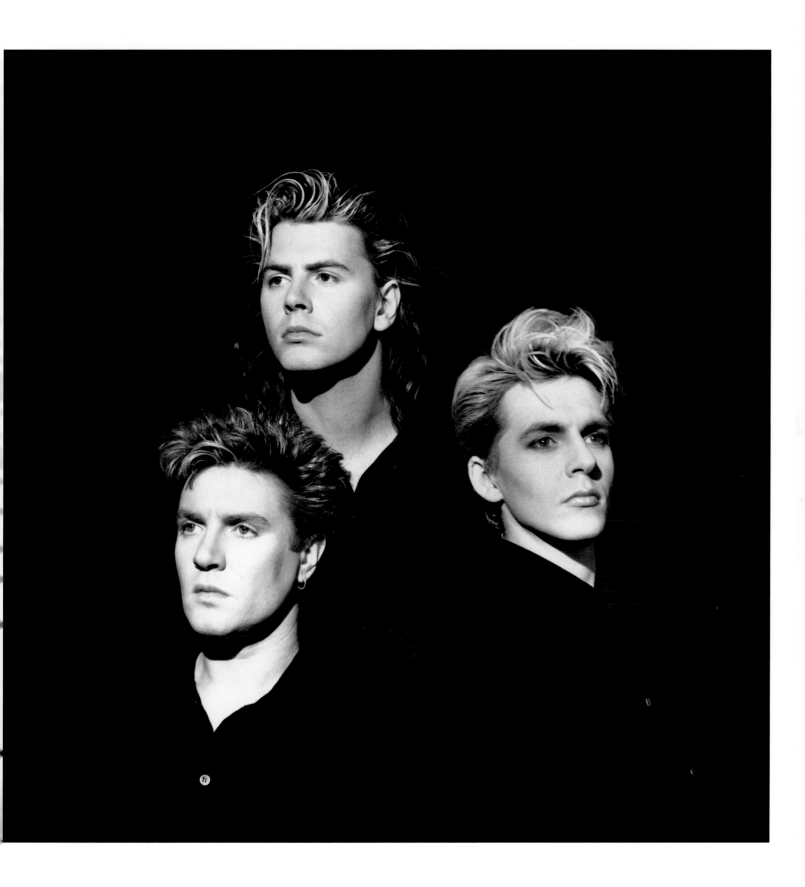

171 Duran Duran, London, 1986

172 Princess Stéphanie of Monaco, New York, 1985

173 Still life, New York, 1988

174 Jerry Hall and Mick Jagger, Barbados, 1986

175 Jerry Hall and Rick, Barbados, 1986

176 Frechey Halston, New York, 1979

177 Bianca Jagger in a design by Halston, New York, 1982

178 Still life, Oyster Bay, Long Island, 1989

179 Andy Warhol, New York, 1984

180 Diana Vreeland, New York, 1979

181 Erté, Barbados, 1986

182 Bruce Weber, New York, 1988

183 Karl Lagerfeld, Paris, 1979

184 Yves Saint Laurent, in his country house near Deauville, 1986

185 Advertisement for Calvin Klein socks, New York, 1983

186 Calvin Klein, in his New York apartment, 1984

187 Perfume advertisement, New York, 1982

188 Perry Ellis fashions, New York, 1982

189 Advertisement for Chanel perfume, New York, 1987

190 Yves Saint Laurent fashions, Paris, 1984

191 Lingerie fashions, New York, 1983

192 Advertisement for Jerbe stockings, Paris, 1985

193 Iman in an evening gown by Valentino, fashion shot, New York, 1982

194 One of Norman Norell's famous Mermaid dresses, New York, 1988

195 Advertisement for stockings, New York, 1987

196 Zoli model agency, New York, 1985

197 Givenchy fashions, Paris, 1985

198 Advertisement for 'Courage' bathing suits, Paris, 1978

199 Mounia, fashion shot, Paris, 1978

200 'Study on ivory', advertisement for Saks, New York, 1982/83

201 Nude with jewelry by Verdura, London, 1989

202 Nude, photographed for an article on ready-to-wear fashions, Paris, 1985

203 Claude Montana fashions, Paris, 1979/80

204 Kathleen Turner, New York, 1984

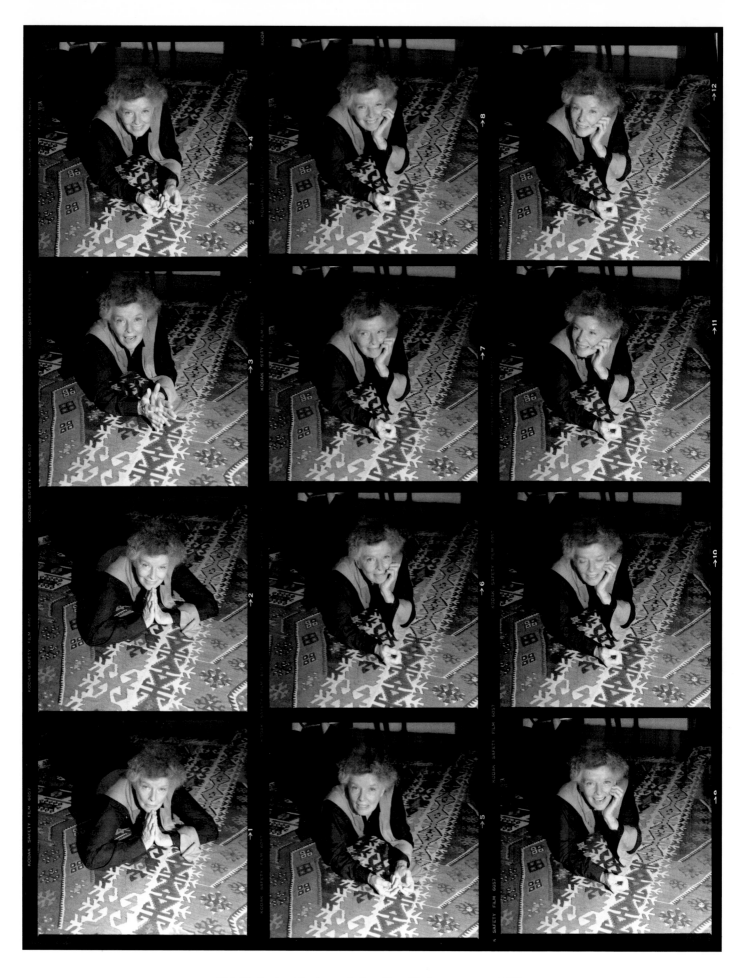

205 Katharine Hepburn, in her New York apartment, 1981

206 Isabella Rossellini, Lancôme advertisement, New York, 1984

207 Calvin Klein fashions, New York, 1983

208 Still life, Lake Como, 1981

BIOGRAPHY

1906 Horst Paul Albert Bohrmann born 14 August in Weissenfels-an-der-Saale, second son of Max Bohrmann and his wife Klara, née Schönbrodt. His father is a wealthy shopkeeper (he runs a thriving hardware business), has wide-ranging interests and is a member of the local Masonic lodge; he later attends the philosopher Graf Keyserling's 'School of Wisdom', founded in Darmstadt in 1920; meets the Indian poet Rabindranath Tagore as well as Josephine Baker.

1913 Horst's mother is admitted temporarily to a sanatorium.

1914 On the outbreak of the First World War, Horst's father is called up to serve on the Western Front, not to return until the end of the war in 1918.

The 1920s The family's financial situation is consolidated quickly after the war; Horst's father is the first in Weissenfels to buy a car. Through his Aunt Grete, whose house in Weimar is a meeting place for numerous artists, Horst meets Eva Weidemann, a student of dance and drama at the Bauhaus. She arouses his interest in avant-garde art; he is soon familiar with the latest developments in dance, theatre, painting and architecture. He spends a year in Switzerland, being treated for a lung disease. In the late '20s Horst begins to study at the Hamburg Kunstgewerbeschule. Friends made there include many sons and daughters of wealthy Hamburg families, such as Mirzel Darboven, daughter of the coffee importer. Horst writes to Le Corbusier, asking him for an apprenticeship in his Paris architectural office. Le Corbusier agrees.

1930 Horst goes to Paris at the beginning of the year to train under Le Corbusier. He makes friends with Robert de Saint-Jean and Julien Green and visits many galleries and museums. He meets *Vogue* photographer Baron George Hoyningen-Huene. He spends the summer in Berlin as the guest of brother and sister Francesco and Eleonora von Mendelssohn; highly cultured and musical, they introduce him to the theatre world. Eleonora plays in the Max Reinhardt Ensemble. Horst meets Gustav Gründgens and Erich Maria Remarque. In the winter he travels to England with Huene. Among others they visit the Ashcombe home of photographer Cecil Beaton, who is working for British *Vogue.*

1931 Horst's association with *Vogue* begins in the spring, thanks to Huene: he introduces him to fashion designer Carl Erickson and his wife, as well as to Dr Mehemed Agha, art director of *Vogue* in New York. Shortly afterwards he begins work as a photographer in *Vogue's* Paris studio. His first photo appears in the French November edition. In the winter he travels to the South of France with Huene.

1932 At the beginning of the year *Vogue* publisher Condé Nast invites Horst to work for him in the USA for six months. He arrives in New York in the spring. Portraits of Bette Davis. Dismissed by Condé Nast before the end of his contract due to differences of opinion. From the autumn he stays for several months in Huene's house in Hammamet, Tunisia. First exhibition in the La Plume d'Or Gallery in Paris; reviewed by Janet Flanner in the *New Yorker.*

1934 In February Horst works in England: photographs of Noel Coward and Yvonne Printemps. Portraits of Lisa Fonssagrives, Natasha Paley, Cole Porter and Elsa Schiaparelli in Paris.

1935 Huene moves to *Harper's Bazaar* at the beginning of the year; Horst takes over his job at *Vogue* in Paris. Soon afterwards Condé Nast invites him back to New York. Short trip to Hollywood; he photographs Katharine Hepburn and George Cukor. His return to Paris is followed by a holiday at Eleonora von Mendelssohn's Austrian home, Schloss Kammer on the Attersee. Returns to New York in the autumn.

1936 Meets Luchino Visconti while staying in Paris at the beginning of the year; start of a lifelong friendship. Holiday at Schloss Kammer with Huene in July; excursion to Venice. Returns to New York in the autumn.

1937 Horst rents an apartment in Sutton Place, New York, with Huene. In the summer he meets Coco Chanel. Holiday at Schloss Kammer in September.

1938 Autumn: Horst's first exhibition in the USA – portraits and fashion photography in Germain Seligman's Art Gallery, New York. In December he photographs Toscanini in New York.

274

1939 Travels to Greece with Huene in the spring. In June Horst meets Thornton Wilder and Jean Cocteau in Paris. In July he stays in Schuls-Tarasp (Engadine, Switzerland) and returns to New York in September. Outbreak of the Second World War.

1940 Horst applies for US citizenship.

1941 11 December: Hitler and Mussolini declare war on the United States.

1942 In the summer Horst passes a medical for the US army. Death of Condé Nast (September). Horst is called up for 15 October, but the order is postponed two days beforehand.

1943 Horst joins the US army on 2 July; his first posting is to Camp Upton, Long Island, followed by basic training in Fort Belvoir, Virginia. 21 October: sworn in on the Constitution of the USA, receives US citizenship as Horst P. Horst. Becomes an army photographer; some of his work is for *Belvoir Castle*, the local forces' magazine.

1944 At the end of the year – while Horst is still stationed in Fort Belvoir – his first book, *Photographs of a Decade*, appears in New York. Work for the weekly magazine *Outfit*, and for *Yank*.

1945 Horst photographs US president Harry S. Truman. Vogue has meantime put together a new team of photographers, including Cecil Beaton and Irving Penn; nevertheless, Horst receives a new contract when he is released from the army. Travels to Mexico.

1946 Horst works for Vogue in Paris. He meets many of his old friends and photographs Gertrude Stein, Léon Blum, Romain Rolland and Oscar Dominguez. Back in New York he continues work on his second book, *Patterns from Nature*, a collection of plant still lifes. Horst's long-cherished plan of building himself a house in Oyster Bay, Long Island, and settling there, takes on concrete shape.

1947 Horst moves into the house in Oyster Bay. Christian Dior, Niki de Gunzburg and Salvador Dali are among the first visitors. In the spring Horst meets British diplomat Valentine Lawford in New York. In the summer he travels to Paris and Venice; he photographs Misia Sert, Jean Cocteau and Jean Marais. Returns to Oyster Bay in September. In the autumn he is visited there by Cecil Beaton. In the winter Horst and Lawford travel through Arizona, New Mexico and Texas to Mexico, Guatemala and Cuba.

1948 Goes to London and Paris. Photographs English country houses.

1949 In July Horst and Lawford travel to Beirut, via London, Venice and Rome. Next stops are Damascus, Dera (Syria), and Baghdad. They go on to Tehran and spend two weeks in Iran, followed by visits to Tel Aviv, Haifa and Jerusalem. Return to Paris, where Horst photographs the latest fashions for *Vogue*. Part of the autumn spent in California.

1950 Second trip to Iran in the spring. In Tehran he meets Lawford, who is working at the British Embassy there. In the region between Chalus and Gurgan, near the Soviet border, they are twice arrested, suspected of spying.

1951 Coco Chanel visits Horst in February in Oyster Bay. American *Vogue* closes down its New York studio; the photographers now work in their own ateliers. Horst rents the apartment previously occupied by the painter Pavel Tchelitchew on the East Side to use as a studio. In December he travels to Rome and Kitzbühel.

1952 In January Horst goes to Berlin, via Munich. He sees his mother for the first time since the war. In February he returns to Paris to photograph the spring fashions for *Vogue*. In March he photographs Suzy Parker in Kitzbühel, then goes on to Rome where he meets Luchino Visconti. An increase in work for *House and Garden*, which started in the late '40s.

1954/55 Horst spends part of each summer in the Tyrol.

1956 Travels to Germany and Austria in the summer.

1957 Numerous advertising contracts in the USA.

1958 Travels to Marrakesh (Morocco) in January. In the summer Horst photographs celebrities and their homes in Germany and Austria, then Manzù and Moravia in Italy. He visits Visconti in Rome. On his way back he photographs Herbert von Karajan in the Tyrol and Ingrid Bergman in Paris. Large exhibitions in the USA: travel photography in the Country Art Gallery, Long Island, and 'Twenty-Five Years of Portraits' in the Sagittarius Gallery, Manhattan.

1959 Advertising shots in Jamaica, Florida and the Bahamas at the beginning of the year. In the spring and summer Horst works in Germany and Austria. In October he buys a mountain farm in the Tyrol.

1960   Advertising work in Florida.   Spends the spring and summer renovating his farm.   In September he returns to New York via Amsterdam.

1961 Diana Vreeland becomes editor-in-chief of American *Vogue*. She spurs Horst on to tackle an entirely new area; series of photos illustrating the lifestyle of international high society become one of his specialities in the '60s, alongside fashion and advertising. From now onwards Horst spends nearly all of his time travelling, on both sides of the Atlantic.

1962 January: advertising photos in Florida and Hawaii. In February Horst sets off on a two-month round-the-world trip: he goes to California, Japan, Hong Kong, Thailand, India, Nepal, Egypt and Rome. The new *Vogue* series begins in August with a photo-report on Consuela Vanderbilt-Balsan, the former Duchess of Marlborough. Death of Horst's mother.

1963 In January Huene visits Horst in Oyster Bay. August: the New York première of Visconti's first film, *The Leopard*. Horst photographs the Rothschilds in Château Mouton, the Windsors in Paris and Emilio Pucci in Florence.

1964   Travels to France, England and Ireland for *Vogue*; in June spends several weeks in Copenhagen working on a special edition on Denmark.

1965 Works in California and Hawaii at the beginning of the year. In February and March he photographs German Baroque and Rococo churches for the next Christmas edition of *Vogue*. Travels to Italy – visits the Agnellis in Piedmont and Cy Twombly in Rome, among others – and England. In December he works in Hawaii.

1966 Horst photographs his own house in Oyster Bay for the *Vogue* series. During the early part of the year he is commissioned by *Vogue* to take photographs on Capri and in Germany, France, Vienna and England. In May he visits Coco Chanel in Paris. He sees her for the last time.

1967 Photos for *Vogue* in – among other places – Venezuela, Portugal, Virginia and Texas.

1968 Publication of *Vogue*'s *Book of Houses, Gardens, People* with photos by Horst and text by Valentine Lawford. Several trips to France and Italy for *Vogue* in the spring/summer. Horst is in Venice when he hears of the death of George Hoyningen-Huene (9 September).

1969 May and June spent in Normandy, Rome and Paris.

1970 Work trips to Guadeloupe and the Bahamas. Horst works on his book, *Salute to the Thirties*, which contains portraits by himself and Huene. It is published a year later.

1971 Coco Chanel dies in January. Diana Vreeland leaves *Vogue*, although her celebrities series continues into the mid-'70s. Horst works in France and Italy. Due to pressure of time he is forced to turn down Visconti's invitation to take the stills during the filming of *Death in Venice*. The next years are taken up chiefly with work for *House and Garden*.

1972 Horst works in Mexico (March) and in France (May). In June he travels to Istanbul and Romania where he photographs many of the old frescoed churches and monasteries in Transsylvania and Wallachia. Later he goes on to Barcelona.

1973 Commissioned by *Vogue*, Horst visits the Rothschilds near Bordeaux and art historian Douglas Cooper in his château in Provence.

1975 January: private trip to Leningrad and Moscow. March: death of Luchino Visconti.

1976 March: exhibition at the Sonnabend Gallery, New York.

1977 Exhibition at the Andrew Crispo Gallery, New York.

1978 Several work trips to France for American *Vogue* and *House and Garden*. In August he spends a week in Greece. In September Horst appears on TV in Hamburg, then goes on to Switzerland. From December once again he photographs Paris *haute couture* for French *Vogue*. Richard J. Tardiff becomes his agent.

1979 Horst works in Santo Domingo (April/May) and Munich (early May). In July/August he photographs Axel Springer in Berlin. In September he travels to Morocco: portraits of Yves Saint Laurent in his house in Marrakesh. In November he takes photos for French *Vogue* in Paris.

1980 In the '80s Horst works for English, Italian and Spanish *Vogue* as well as for their American and French counterparts; and also now for *Vanity Fair*. Exhibitions at the Neikrug and Staley Wise Galleries in New York.

1981-83 Horst works on two books.

1982 The Staley Wise Gallery becomes Horst's gallery in New York.

1984 In October Valentine Lawford's biography *Horst. His Work and his World* is published, followed, a few weeks later, by James Watters' book, *Return Engagement*, with Horst's portraits of famous film actresses. Several exhibitions in New York, including retrospective in the International Center of Photography.

1985 May-July: the 'Horst – Photography 1931-84' exhibition in the Fortuny Palace, Venice. Richard J. Tardiff becomes Horst's manager.

1986 August: exhibition at the Hamilton Gallery in London.

1987 Exhibitions at the Stadtmuseum, Munich (September-November) and the Kunsthalle, Bremen (November 1987-January 1988).

1988 Numerous exhibitions: in London (Hamilton's), Frankfurt (Fotografie Forum), Zurich (Nikon Live Galerie), Hamburg (Museum für Kunst und Gewerbe). Horst receives the Lifetime Achievement Award of the Council of Fashion Designers of America. Exhibition at the Jane Corkin Gallery, Toronto (October).

1989 In April Horst receives an honorary doctorate from the University of Bradford. Exhibitions at Hamilton's in London, the Fahey/Klein Gallery in Los Angeles (May) and the Holly Solomon Gallery, New York (July).

1990 Exhibitions at the Galleria in Houston, Texas (February) and the Jane Corkin Gallery, Toronto (October). Exhibition of platinum prints of his photos from 1935 to 1989 in the Fay Gold Gallery, Atlanta, Georgia (December 1990-January 1991).

1991 Preparations for an exhibition to be held from March to September in the Musée des Arts de la Mode in the Louvre.